Up from the *Ashes*

Poetry & Prose for the Soul

by

Carolyn Kristos French

Ark House Press
arkhousepress.com

All Bible references are from the New King James Spirit Filled Life Bible.
Copyright 1991 Thomas Nelson, Inc.

Cataloguing in Publication Data:
Title: Up from the Ashes
ISBN: 978-1-7643052-0-4 (pbk)
Subjects: REL012040 RELIGION / Christian Living / Inspirational; REL077000 RELIGION / Faith; POE003000 POETRY / Subjects & Themes / Religious.

Design by initiateagency.com

Thank you to my granddaughter Breanna, for the drawings.
I love and appreciate you very much.

Table of Contents

Preamble

I sing Hallelujah. This is part 2 of my attempt to paint a word picture of my struggle coming out of the emotional and mental pain of abuse, plus keeping my faith in Christ at the same time. Part 1 is found in my book, *Explosion of Hope, Poetry & Prose for the Soul.*

At the time of writing this section of poems, I was having and completing 2 years of counselling with a psychologist. Immediately after this, my beautiful second husband David, was diagnosed with cancer. It was like, I went from the frying pan into the fire. He died 6 months later. Following this, abuse from family was thrown at me and I ended up in a very dark place for a number of years.

But, praise God, He has brought me through and up from the ashes of my life. No matter what I have been through, I have always found the Lord God Almighty to be my Rock, my Fortress. He is the only One that I found trustworthy during a time when I did not know who to trust.

If you identify with anything written in this book, I urge you to call out for help. The Lord Jesus Christ will be with you as you work through the issues troubling you.

Blessings on your journey,

Carolyn Kristos French

The Spirit of the Lord God is upon me because the Lord has anointed me to preach good tidings to the poor. He has sent Me to heal the broken hearted (shattered in heart and mind), to proclaim liberty to the captives, and the opening of the prison to those who are bound. To proclaim the acceptable year of the Lord, and the day of vengeance of our God. To comfort all who mourn, to console those who mourn in Zion. To give them beauty for ashes, the oil of joy for mourning, the garment of praise for the spirit of heaviness, that they may be called trees of righteousness, the planting of the Lord, that He may be glorified.

Isaiah 61:1-3

Words in brackets are my own

The Cross

It was at the cross where I encountered the Light.
It was at the cross where Jesus gave me the right
To become a child of His, in whom He could delight.

No better place there is to be, than at the cross, on my knee
To hear my Saviour say 'Come, you beloved of My Father,
Enter in and be seated – you are My great treasure'.

No better place have I found. No other place is Holy ground.
The blood stained ground on which My Saviour bled,
As upon that cruel tree He hung – then He bowed His head.

"It is finished!' I heard Him cry, and then He died
For me, for you - salvation He did buy.
I rest my case in Him alone, for He, my sin, did own.

No other Name - no other place – did He secure my grace.
My sins are gone. I've been set free
Since I bowed my knee at Calvary.

No other Name, but the Name of Jesus Christ my Lord.
No other Name could ever afford the price
Of my redemption from curse and vice.

'Twas at the cross where I first encountered the Light
And the Light continues on, shining brighter every day.
I wend my way to that cross and discover
That Jesus is The Way.

He is my Way – He is my Light
The Truth unveiled – the Truth revealed
But only at the cross.

**

Jesus and Me

In the night watches when I am alone,
Jesus comes near me - to tell me - I am His own.
No matter what happens, no matter what goes,
Jesus is with me, as He only knows.
My nights, they are long. My tears they are dry.
When Jesus appears, that's when I cry.
My thoughts are bound up, locked up far away.
But Jesus comes near, and my fear does allay.

I know who I am, but something is wrong.
Satan attacks me when I am alone.
My Jesus, I cry - Come to my aid!
The day is approaching, and Satan is nigh.
At once, in a flash, Jesus appears.
His Light everlasting wipes all of my tears.
Satan is gone and I am at rest.
For all through my life, Jesus knows best.

***

God's Special Word

For you shall not go out to the right or left, but straight ahead, heeding what I shall say to you – not listening to the whispers of the enemy when he says, go here, go there.

I am the Lord Who leads you forward. My path is straight, not devious. I will take you forward in the power of My Name. My Name is pure and holy. My Name is full of glory. I am Jesus Christ Who saves you, and heals you, and leads you into My Promised Land – Who lifts up your head and transforms you. Stay in Me, and do not deviate from the path I have set before you. Satan would ensnare you even in the last minute, so pay attention to My Word and keep safe.

I will not leave any stone unturned in My pursuit of you. I will seek you and seal you as My own. I have spoken! I have decided to walk with you and trust you with My Heart. I will show you My Heart at a time you least expect, and you will be most surprised. Keep your focus and I will keep you to the end, and the gates of Hell will not prevail against you. I am Alpha and Omega.

Come to Me with a willing heart to seek My face and My infilling. I will not fail to pour out My Living Waters and overflow you. Your deserts shall become streams of water and the jackals shall no longer live there. Love, passionate love I give you. Joy, overflowing joy I give you.

Your land shall flow with laughter and the burden of the ox shall be lifted off and be gone permanently. I have spoken!

Do not fear the voices – do not fear their faces, for I will obliterate them from your heart and mind. Keep surrendering to Me – keep focus on Me. I am the One who delivers you from Pharaoh and his minions. I will break him early in the morning and again at noonday. At twilight you will see him no more. I AM will deliver you.

Keep pleading the Blood of Jesus over your household, and at daybreak you shall go out with joy, with much joy, and everlasting peace will be yours. The past bondage will end soon. Keep focus – Keep the faith – Do not lose heart. I am with you. I have not forgotten all you have believed for.

Even though the enemy seeks stronger holds over you, like Job, you will come through, and I will restore double to you – double the brightness of My Glory – double the peace and joy – double for your trouble. I will not fail to deliver My promise to you – only keep the faith – keep the focus for a bit longer, and all will be well.

I know you have little strength, but I am holding you safe in the palm of My hand. I am the One who brightens your day. I love you so much more than you realize. I am God Almighty, Maker of Heaven and Earth. I made you and I will keep you.

Amen and Amen and Amen.

***

Jesus and the Past

My dead lung, it sat up on a tree.
It sits for all and sundry. It sits for all to see.
It's a symbol of my past which has broken right away,
And it came to pass just the other day.
It is looking so forlorn, as by itself it sits.
It sits upon my Saviour's cross, just as He hung that day.
My Saviour, He has carried all my sins away.
My past, so filthy dirty – He makes me clean today.

His love is like a rainbow which shines from up above.
He went to that cross because of His great love
For me, and all the others who have a dirty past.
A past so unforgiving, it left us in a trance.
But Jesus came and broke the power of all that sin and death.
He did this on the cross, when He gave out His last breath.
'Twas Jesus who did die for me, and He died for you
Who had such a rotten life – to make your life brand new.

'Tis Jesus on the cross - my sin on Him is laid.

My past it cannot stay, for all my sins are paid.

The 'Word', it says, my past has died, and now new life begins.

It is my blessed Saviour who gives to me my grin.

For Jesus, I have promised to take Your heart on board,

And now because I've done this, I have a great reward.

My life is now turned around. I found a brand new way.

His Name is Jesus Christ, who I met the other day.

***

My Story

My Story is not ended here
I am still alive to tell the tale
Of Jesus' mercy and His grace
To His little child.

I am not one of high renown
I have travelled through life's sewer
But God's own love
Denies me never.

I have much spot and wrinkle
Caused by so much pain
But Jesus is my Lord
He is my only gain.

I will not deny my past
It isn't very pretty
But God Almighty washed me clean
And made all things to fit His scheme.

My life has a new beginning
Kith and kin are coming home
The truth is out – the lies are gone
His will be done as I recline.

I fall into His loving arms
He cares for me so much
But I am at a loss
As to how to share this much.

The riches in my life are many.
The sanctity of life, lived in a special way.
The grace of God from day to day,
The freedom to move within that grace
The freedom to face each day
Knowing He is leading the way.

***

The Promise

In death there is life, even though we can't see it.
In death there is joy, e'en though we can't feel it.
For just as the sunshine follows the rain,
So My Spirit comes, in the midst of your pain.

My Life within you feels your pain.
My Life within you sees what gain
Can be accomplished through the pain.
There is nothing to do but work it through.
My Life within you, will see you through.

The clouds of sorrow and grief are there.
Put your tomorrows into My safe care.
My care will provide all that you need
When the nights are so long
And the days never end.

My Spirit will comfort and collect all your tears,
And pour out again, the joy of the years
Spent with your loved one, and laughter will come
As you remember the love of that special one.

As you go from here, it is a dark space,
But light shall return to its rightful place.
The clouds will lighten. The load will lift.
The night become dawn, and the sun will shine.

My Spirit is with you. I know where you're at,
So go on living, and, in return,
My Promise of help in your time of need,
To never forsake you, and never leave
Still stands in this, your hour of need.

***

Written for someone mourning their spouse

Where Were You?

Where were you on the day I was crucified?
Where were you on the day I died?
Were you in your comfortable chair
Sitting by the fireside?

Where were you when I poured out my soul?
Where were you when I gave My all?
Were you watching down the road
Thinking you might see something to behold?

Were you there in Gethsemane
When My tears flowed down My cheek?
Were you there on that road
As I carried the cross? Such a heavy load!

Were you there when I died for you?
Can you see what I went through?
It was for you – I took your place.
You were the one full of disgrace.

But, my Lord, I did not know
All that You would go through
To bring me out – to bring me in
To set me free from all my sin.

My sin, it is so bad.
It bothers me day and night.
Lord, where was I on that fateful day
When You were crucified?

You were right there in front of Me.
I saw you from afar.
My loving eyes did seek you out
As you tried to hide from Me.

A loving look, a tender gaze
From Jesus Christ my Lord,
Is what it took to draw me in,
When He was crucified.

The anguish on His face as He took my disgrace,
It pains me to the core.
To think that He would die for me, to take my place
So He could set me free.

But now, some 2000 years have past
Since that fateful day
When Christ, the Son of God was hung
Upon a rugged tree.
That tree, which formed a cross
On which my Saviour died
Still stands as a witness
Of Jesus' love for me.

***

The Mercy Seat

It is well with my soul, I heard my Saviour say
As He passed by, just the other day.
He stopped to chat – to say I was His own.
I bowed before Him, as on the mercy seat, He sat down.

I saw His loving look, as upon me He did gaze.
He seemed in no hurry to rush away this day.
Our meeting was not chance. He had planned it long ago
That we would meet together, on this most glorious day.

He's a loving Saviour who calls me safely home.
He's a loving Saviour who would make me His own.
He's a loving Saviour who sets the captive free.
He's a loving Saviour is what He is to me.

My Saviour, He is strong. He is the great I Am.
He is my all in all, from Heaven's Almighty Realm.
He gives to me His pledge – a promise rich and fair.
I give to Him my love and I give to Him my care.

My Saviour, He does listen as I chat away to Him.
He is very interested, in all my kith and kin.
He promises to touch my world
With the heat of His great love,
As we quietly sit together on this, His mercy seat.

I love to meet Him on this mercy seat.
It is a place of refuge when I want to be alone.
It is a place of mercy that I found long time ago,
When I was still awandering
With no place else to go.

The mercy of my God and King
Whose love was poured right down,
Is still my place of refuge
When things go upside down.

***

My Journey

It was many years ago when a man his wife did know,
Within a week of that day –
Her every dream was snatched away.
Her dream of love without condition – her dream that life
Would be so bright – it was as though, out went the light.

The years they did come and go,
And life was filled with lots of woe.
Home life was a mess –
The children also felt the stress
Of abuse, and this caused all of us distress.

We went from place to place, but still the same disgrace
We could never, seem to displace.
The years have come and gone – the family is extended
But unity has yet to be reclaimed.

I suffer, I am told, from Post Traumatic Stress.
It comes from many years of stuffing down my chest,
All the abuse and ill treatment of which I could not speak
For fear of retaliation – I tried to do my best.

But things have a habit of returning to the surface
At times when least expected –
In ways totally unexpected.
Panic attacks and irrational fears –
Triggers of sights, and sounds
And smells, people and places –
Overwhelm me on those days.

I have to deal with the shame of being a battered wife,
Battered emotionally, mentally and spiritually.
No wonder I find it difficult to lead a normal life.

But I found a Friend Who is loyal – One Who treats me kindly.
One Who listens to my cries. He says to me 'Daughter, come,
You are precious to Me – I will heal your heart and mind.

So, I came to Jesus overloaded and sad.
I found in Him a special place and He made me glad.
I am glad Jesus listens as I unburden my heart.
I am glad Jesus cries with me, as I speak of my hurt.

My journey is long, and my heart heals slowly.
But Jesus my Lord is working within me.
In Jesus I stand fully healed and free.
But some days it seems I'm in darkness again.

Each day I am stronger as my heart it does heal.
I cannot afford to look back, but go forward.
But to go forward, I must look back
And acknowledge my pain, my suffering, my shame.

In facing the truth, I am set free.
In facing my past, I realize
I am the person I am today
Because of what happened back there.
I now have a strength, I had not before.
I now have some wisdom and understanding.

I hung onto Jesus and I gave Him my all.
Jesus and me, we talk all the time.
He tells me His secrets and I tell Him mine.
He and I together, we make a great team
And I will go forward proclaiming His Name.

***

God's Secret

There is a secret in God's own heart.
A secret which He wants to impart
Into a heart, receptive and clean,
O Lord make it mine – I don't want to be mean.

I want to be rich with the secrets of God.
To treasure them always and then to impart
These same secrets to others I know,
So that the secret in me begins to show.

What is the secret? You may ask.
A special place? A special thought?
It is that God imparts His blessings
From the heart of Heaven.

It is the secret of His Presence – a hiding place,
A place of prayer – a place of rest,
A place where nothing can molest.
A place where love and mercy flow,
A safe place where I can grow.

It is a secret, O so special,
God gives to those who seek His heart.
It is a secret, so divine,
That Christ alone can give to us
The keys to bring His Presence in.

The secret came as a Baby. He is the Lord of Lords.
He is my all in all, when the world around me falls.
He takes away my grief, my sorrow and my pain,
As I yield and consecrate myself, to Him again this day.

***

Storytime

It was just in time for Christmas,
And all through the house
Was the snore of those sleeping,
And the cat and the mouse.

But high in the sky was a rustling of wings
As angels assembled to have a great sing.
In a stable outback on a cold winter's night
A Baby was born, Who just couldn't wait.

The angels, they sang, with hearts full of joy,
For the Child Who arrived, was a baby Boy.
And the shepherds who heard the great furore,
Rushed to the stable, the Child to adore.

The Child, He grew, as a refugee
Who fled into Egypt to escape a decree,
A decree which caused many children to die,
But God, by His grace, kept this One alive.

Back to His homeland, He came again
To settle and work with a carpenter's plane.
His hands, they were rough, His face, so kind,
The Boy, now a Man, moved into His plan.

The teaching He gave – the miracles wrought,
Was His way of showing the greatness of God.
The plan to redeem us, was His plan all along
When He went to the cross with sorrowful song.

The angels were silent – not one rustle of wings
As they watched our dear Lord take all of our sins.
But the story is told an angel appeared
On the day Jesus rose and conquered the grave.

Hallelujah! They shout! Hallelujah! Amen!
Yours is the glory – all conquering King.

**

All Will Be Well!

All will be well, I heard my heart say,
But my physical reaction went the other way.
All will be well, I heard my Lord sing
But my physical reaction recoiled again.

How do I connect my heart and my head?
How do I make things come into alignment?
I read the Word. I pray every day
And yet my faith seems to fly away.

The trauma of youth – the things which were done
Seem less likely, me to overcome.
My faith, it has grown to conquer it all
But my head and my heart don't agree overall.

The pain and the grief are slowly fading
And the joy of the morning is slow in returning
But God has decreed an end to this mess
And He has decreed I am to be blest.

I take my Lord's Word as gospel today.
I look at it clearly in light of this day.
His Word is so true. It's hard to believe
My head and my heart do disagree.

So, into submission, I bring my mind.
My heart, soul and body to Him belong.
My Lord and my God, I proclaim once again
As I kneel at the cross and confess all my sin.

His forgiveness and healing, they wash me again
As on my knees, time with Him I spend.
I arise, to stand on the faith of my Lord
As I take to His Book and believe every Word.

***

Love Your Enemies???

Love your enemies, I hear the Lord say.
Love my enemies? There is no way.
I want them dead to relieve my pain.
To have them live, what is the gain?
Long life, happiness? The list goes on,
But how long on earth can this go on?

I see my Saviour's arms stretched wide.
It was for them that He did die.
It was for me, I know so well,
But why should they not go to hell?
They did me wrong down through the years
And they did cause me lots of tears.

But Christ has called me to His side
To be like Him and so abide
In love, and kindness, truth and care,
So I could be like Him and share
The greatest story ever told
So love like His, others would behold.

The tension of this life is great
To love my Lord and then behold
At the gate, my enemy so bold.
My heart cannot withstand this tension
Something must give or melt away.
My heart must rest in Christ alone,
To pray for those I'd rather disown.

So on my knees I bow to my King
To serve Him always, has such a great ring,
But to obey and be like Him
Will chastise my heart and cause me to sing
Hallelujah! What a Saviour! My Redeemer!
Friend of sinners so bad
Jesus went to the cross and there He died.

But, up from the grave He arose
And He, His enemies deposed.
His conquering power o'er sin He proclaimed
So life could be lived in His Holy Name.
But I struggle to rise to be like Him.
I, once an enemy, am now His friend.
He calls me His own – for my life He atoned.

To be like Him, my heart cries out,
But the tension of life is all about
Forgiving and loving those you want out,
Out of your life and out of your house,
So again on my knees, I am crying again
Lord, give me some help to be free of this pain.

My child, He replies, I had compassion for you
When I laid down my Life on the cross.
Now it's your turn to carry the Light of My Love
To those you would rather not.
My love, it is deep – it covers your sin
My love, so deep – will cover their sin.

So be not afraid of their sin, nor your pain.
I will carry you once again
And you will know joy and the peace of My heart,
As on this journey you make a start.
Pray for their lives, their souls, their heart.
I will be with you – thus bringing the healing
To your broken heart.

***

My Saviour

So here we are – we are right here. His love is pouring down.
I see my Saviour on the cross. His arms outstretched to me.
I see His loving eyes – they are so full of pain
And yet, His purpose, undenied – upon that cross He died.

I see that cruel cross – so barbaric,
And yet, for mankind's sin it stands.
It is a sign of man's cruel acts,
For which my Saviour died.

My Saviour, He does see me as I view Him from afar.
He beckons me to come and put my finger
Where a hole was made into His heart
To make my own heart whole.

We did a swap, my Saviour and I.
He died so I could live.
He was wounded so I could be healed.
The hole in His heart made by the sword
Fills up my heart with the Sword of His Word.

I hear the bells a'ringing. These bells, they toll for me.
They invite me into His presence, and,
From the towers of Heaven, they sing
'Ever onward, ever upward' – I hear my Saviour call,
'Come unto Me when weary and I will fill your soul".

***

Birthday Celebrations

Think of all the changes you've seen
The places you've been
The people you've met
And the family beget.

Think of God's grace
And blessings untold
That He would allow you
To get this old.

Think of the friends who love you this day
Think of family who are far away
Think of God's goodness
As mercies unfold on your way.

Think of His love
As you go through this day
And say 'thank You'
For all He has done
On this, your 90th birthday.

***

My Lord – My Love

He is the awesome morning star
He is most beautiful to my soul
He is my Lover, my Peace, my All.
He is the One who lights my way
He is the One who brightens my day
He is the fairest of them all.

My Lord, He sits on high
Above all other things and
He is the Lord of all my heart
And to His love I sing.
An offering most rare, He brings to me
His love, unblemished by anything.

My Lord, He comes to me
In the darkest of my night
We share sweet fellowship
In the presence of His light.
His light does radiate His warmth
As only He can do.
He wraps me in His love
And banishes my fears.

My Lord, the One to whom I owe
A debt so great, that only He can know.
Yet, He forgives my debt
And bestows upon my heart
A love, so fresh, and life so real
That He, Himself, imparts.

His mercy never ends, but extends
To me, His child, who has broken all the rules.
To me, His child, forgiveness flows
And His grace begins to overflow.

***

Knowing Him

Am I a little butterfly sitting by Your Throne?
Am I a roaring lion, one that you must tame?
You know my every moment as I come before Your Name.
You know the hairs upon my head and the colour of my mane.

I came to know You as a child and ever since that day
You had Your hand upon me, whatever came my way.
I see Your hand of mercy. I see Your hand of grace,
But I seek Your eyes, as I look into Your face.

To know Your face is shining upon this child so small,
You see my every movement when I am trying to be bold.
You see me when I flounder in every twist and turn,
And You speak 'well done' to me at every step I learn.

Lord, please confirm to me, the way that I must take.
Everything around me is beginning to make me shake.
Things are happening fast, and I am struggling to behold
Just how this little child of yours has now become so bold.

Bold enough, O Lord, to take You at Your Word,
To see the open doors, You are starting to unfold.
Doors which once were shut, now seem to be wide open,
And I stand in awe and worship,
Of the King Who made it happen.

You are my blessed Saviour. You are the King of Kings.
You have called me to Your Kingdom for such a time as this.
You have lifted my head above my foes, as only You can do,
And I bow in awe and worship of the One, Who loves me so.

***

Joyful Love

My enemies are gone. I have now been told.
My future is bright and cheery as my destiny unfolds.
My Saviour speaks His Word, and the Glory of His Light
Fills my heart with joy, just like broad daylight.

My Saviour, He is good. My Saviour, He is kind.
He fills my every longing and makes my face to shine.
His goodness and His mercy upon me now He rains,
As dew drops fall from Heaven and become torrential rain.

His Glory shines and all around me now
Such love beyond all measure, begins to fill my soul.
The love He gives is priceless, abounding all the more
As I give to Him the honour, He is my all in all.

He shines upon me from the north,
The south, the east, the west.
He is all encompassing, for He knows what is best.
His love is like the rainbow after a big, bad storm,
And His love is also blessing me when I feel forlorn.

I cannot take my eyes off Him, nor do I want to do
Anything that hurts Him, or brings His Name to shame.
I must give to Him my best – nothing less,
For He gave His all for me – which was His very best.

The Lord, He is my God – the one and only ever
The Giver of my joy – the Lifter of my head
He is my all in all – no one else will do
And I give my love to Him and to Him I say, 'I do'.

***

My Aching Heart

In the middle of the night when I can't sleep so tight
I hear my Saviour calling me to Him.
Up out of bed I come, to meet with Him alone.
His door is always open. The light is always on
And His presence fills my very lonely heart.
I cast my cares to Him – an offering do I bring
Even though I can't reveal my every thought.

My heart is aching for my children. They are so far away
Locked in their own little world, of sorrow, grief and pain.
My heart, it wants to break. My heart, it wants to cry
And I wish there was some thing I could do
To break the silence I must keep, until they all come through.

My heart cries out 'O Lord please come
And fill my aching void'.
Your kingdom come - Your will be done
In me and mine, as it is in Heaven.
My soul, it rests in Christ alone, for He does all things well.
The day will come when Christ shall come
And get my children out of hell.

***

The City of our God

In the City of our God there are lots of things
Things which money cannot buy.
Things which are without reserve
Things which do apply.
Things of life and joy and peace
Things which God will not deny.
Hope and peace and charity,
These are those which do apply.

His hope, it lifts our spirits high.
His joy, which make us feel sky high,
His love, like a fountain overflows.
His peace, like a river flows.
His light, which shatters all our pain,
His eyes have softness like the gentle rain.

The City of our God, it is the place to be.
In the City of our God, is where I want to be.
His love, like the rainbow, crowns my steps each day,
And I am blessed to be His daughter every single day.

***

The Family Circle

Will the family circle be unbroken
When the day of reckoning comes?
Will we be in that place when we meet Jesus face to face?
Will the day be full of grace and the morning sun so bright
As we meet Jesus at the pearly gate?

At the dawning of that day, will our family circle be there
To meet us just inside, as the glory of the Heavens
Becomes visible to our naked eye?
Will the Light of God shine upon us there,
As with arms outstretched, He welcomes us with care?

To answer all these questions, we need to step aside
To listen with our hearts, to Jesus walking by.
He is looking for a friend. He wants to be our Friend.
A Friend to those whose hearts are open, to let Him enter in.
So on this very day, as we walk along the way,
Let us walk with Jesus, to find a brand new day.

***

My Bed

It is the middle of the night and I am wide awake.
My thoughts go here. My thoughts go there,
As I lay upon my bed.

I think of others as I pray. My thoughts go to and fro,
But God almighty knows the way, all my thoughts should go
As I lay upon my bed.

I want to go to sleep – to sleep upon my bed
But sleep eludes me as I turn
And toss upon my bed.

***

Journey of Hope

It's such a little thing in the overall scheme of things
But to us, it's like we have no wings.
No wings to fly above the storm – no wings to fly at all.
The clouds are black – our vision dim,
But all the while we trust in Him.

Peace flows like a river on a balmy day,
But in my soul, it is stormy here today.
Where is the peace, My Lord, I cry,
As to my knees I frequently fly.
I seek His face as oft I can,
But my soul is tormented, and I feel alone.

My daughter, He says, all will be well.
I have ordained to make you quite well.
The load is heavy. I know very well.
Please follow My footsteps out of your hell.
The place of desire for much better things,
Is on My agenda and to you I will sing.

I will sing of My grace, and I will sing of My love.
For you, my sweet daughter, are one whom I love.
My love will constrain you. My love will detain you.
My love is strong and compelling.
My song I will sing over you in the night,
My song I will sing also in daylight.

I hold you in the palm of My hand.
I will carry you right through this land,
This land of pain – this land of grief.
I am the One, Who brings you relief.
The Light will come – the pain be gone,
As you follow My footsteps over terrain
Which leads to new joy and hope again.

***

Adopting a Son

How does one adopt a son?
A son who breaks your heart
A son, whose life has torn you apart
A son for whom Christ died.

How does one love a son
When he steals your life away?
How can his heart, be knit to yours today?
A son for whom Christ died.

How do I love a son
When my heart is breaking so?
As he keeps my daughter from me
And keeps to what he knows.

Lord, I don't have it in me
To love him like You do.
You need to change my heart
So I can love him too.

***

My Need

I feel like I am all alone – alone in all my dreams
And yet my Saviour passes by – His dreams to me unknown.
I walk this earth by faith – my destination sure.
I know I will my dreams fulfil – it is My Master's will.

It is His will to save so many – and healing is His will,
But my eyes, they seem so clouded as I seek to do His will.
I try in vain to do my best when I really need to stop
And listen to His heart which beats when mine does not.

I need to seek His face – to listen to His words,
To follow in His footsteps and tread wherever He leads.
I need Him to brighten up my day as dreary clouds unfold.
I need the sunshine of His love to fill my life each day.

I need to have a special place for Him within my heart.
I need a special grace to see me through this day.
I need His loving kindness to help me overcome
My tendency to cry whenever things are drear.
I need His very presence when life grows strangely dim.
I need His resurrection power so I can live for Him.

***

Decision Time

Now moving right along – one year down the track
From things that have happened – we are not turning back.
Our goal in life is this – to bring the future on
To a place where God will move, the ever moving throng.
People who are lost – people who are sick –
People filled with grief and with life beyond compare.
A people who must seek the Saviour's shining face
To see His majesty and glory, and thereby find relief.

It is so very hard to fathom all the love
The Saviour has in store for us as we wait out all our days.
The time that is allotted is threescore years and ten
And yet, when the Saviour tarries in calling us above
Our lives must be exemplary to those who follow on.

There is a time to live. There is a time to die.
This is the time to follow Him – and no one can deny
The opportunity is given as His heart cries out for them.
But those of us still living, must choose to follow Him.
For once our days are over, there is no other day
To make that one decision, which should be made today.

Our lives do make a difference to those we meet each day,
Whether in our own home or out along the way.
The day to live is now. The day to catch is here.
Either we will live with Him or see the Saviour's tears
As we meet Him face to face and we hear Him say to us
'You did not want Me on the earth,
Now I don't want you here'.
'Lord have mercy, let me in' I say to Him
But He does not know me, as I never let Him in
To my life when I was on the earth
And now because of this, I am consigned to hell.

***

Jesus and Me in Eternity

The days are long, the nights are dark,
But I am still within your heart.
I know you do not understand how much I still command.
I know your pain. I know your grief.
I am the One Who brings relief.
I am the One Who still decides,
The length of times and the length of days.

Your loved one did decide to come and live with Me.
He took My hand and I took his and lifted him into Eternity.
He now can run. He now can fish. He now is really alive.
His sorrow gone, his pain relieved,
His joy increased as he reigns with Me.

He leaves behind his love to share with those who mourn.
I mix My love with his, as well as My concern.
To those he leaves behind, he has a word for you.......

'Do not lose faith. Do not lose heart. I chose a better path.
You asked the Lord for me, and I gave to Him my troth.
I told Him I would come, as I stepped out of my 'boat'.
My 'boat' I leave behind. It is no longer needed.

My new body is so smart. It is all I ever wanted.
Mourn for me and cry for me, but always do remember
I am the one who chose to leave.
The cross I carried is gone. I am set free.

I can remember pain no longer.
Rejoice with me. I am set free.
My Saviour God I see.
He is my all in all. He is not a stranger.
You know Him too and will remember
All He's done for me and you.

Get ready to meet me here when the time, it comes your way.
I'll be waiting here for you on that great and glorious day'.

***

Life's Journey

My God, My God, I cried, as I lay upon my bed.
Such Love, such Love, I cried, as I stood to my feet.
Ours is not to understand the why's
And wherefores of this land.
Ours is to live and not to falter,
As we make our way to Heaven yonder.

My God, My God, I cry.
Grant me a wish before I die,
That I may live – that I may sing
The praises of my Heavenly King.

I do not understand why life has been so hard
And yet, by His great grace, I am still alive.
Alive to tell the tale of God's great love for me,
That He would take my place on that accursed tree.

Life is a journey – that is for sure,
O'er rocky mountain ranges and of sand upon seashore.
The valleys can be dark – the stream so crystal clear,
The sun so bright – the night so dark,
When stars do not appear.

I want to see my Saviour's face and hear His voice so dear.
I want to stand in His great grace and see everything so clear.
But life has many twists and turns – one thing is for sure,
My Saviour takes me by the hand and makes me feel secure.

His ways I do not understand, but I know His love is great.
He wraps me up in arms of love and gathers up my tears.
My tears they are so many, and yet there's room for more.
My tears they flow like rain drops upon the desert floor.

My life has been so empty and now is getting filled,
As others gather round me to make my life so full.
I need capacity to receive the love so freely given,
So I empty out my soul of all I have forgiven.

I need a place to store the love so it can overflow.
As love flows in and love flows out, it cleanses all my soul.
It reaches to the lost, those hurting and in pain,
And then love does amazing things,
It brings me healing in Jesus' Name.

***

Fire and Gold

I have loved you with an everlasting love,
A love that will not let you go.
I have placed over you a covering,
A sound that echoes like the ring
Of bells so clear and bright and clean.

These bells of Mine, they shine like gold
So beautiful to behold.
Bells so rich and oh so rare,
They like Solomon do glare,
Providing light and sound so pure
None other can anyone procure.

The fire that burns within My heart
Is just for you, My own sweetheart.
The fire glows and brings you warmth
To fill your emptiness of heart.

I have not forgotten the promises I made
When you were young and unafraid.
You marched right on, expecting much
The likes of which require a touch
Of God's Own Hand – the Master's Touch.

Wait and see, He says to me. Just wait and see.
I'm not finished with you yet.
The end is somewhere down the road.
Along the way, you will see – a great deal more of Me.

***

Good Dream – Bad Dream

There is a good dream flowing alongside a bad dream. The dreams are flowing parallel yet interwoven as one seeks to take over the other. One seeks to diminish the other. One seeks to rise above the other. These are the workings of my life. One dream is full of abuse, threats, menace, depression, anxiety and such like. The other dream is full of hope, joy, deliverance and the promise of a future without the other dream. Yet, which shall I choose? Which dream will surrender without a fight? Which dream has enough power behind it to conquer the other? This is my life.

This is the universe within me. I know which one I want to choose. Yet, I am tired, weary of the constant fight. It makes no sense, yet it does make sense. The rivals within and the rivals without are at constant war and I am caught in the middle. Both dreams want me, yes even desire me, but the battle also has the power to bring me to my knees. I have nowhere else to go. I must submit to the good dream. The bad dream must submit to the good dream. I must take and hold fast to the good dream otherwise my life means nothing. My life would end in darkness. Good dream, I choose you and ask that you overwhelm and swallow up the bad dream. Take the bad dream away so I can live in the good dream all my life, or at least what's left of it.

***

Though He slay me, yet will I trust Him. Even so, I will defend my own ways before Him. He also shall be my salvation, for a hypocrite could not come before him.

Job 13:15,16 NKJV

Lord Hear My Heart

My heart cries out to You – Blessed be Your Name
My heart cries out to You – I want to see Your fame
My heart cries out to You – I am in a spot of bother

My heart cries out to You – I give to You my hand
My heart cries out to You – Lord I cannot stand
My heart cries out to You – Lord I need Your power
My heart cries out to You – Sanctify me Lord, in this very hour.

My heart cries out to You – I am in this place of rest
My heart cries out to You –
My soul is unhealthy, tired and stressed
My heart cries out to You – Lord I plead with you
My heart cries out to You – Your face I long to see
My heart cries out to You – Open doors for me

I long to see my Saviour even when at rest.
I long to see my Saviour especially when I'm stressed.
The years have come and gone – My David is at peace.
But I am not. I'm so stressed out. Lord, I need Your peace,
Peace of heart and mind, soul and body too.
I look to You for healing, help and kindness too.
I have become withdrawn with crying in my bones.
Lord, hear my prayer, as I cry out to You.

I know Your ways are right, but justice is my plea.
I need Your mercy in this land of weeping night and day.
I know that You are with me. My future is secure,
But right now, in my life, I want the praises to resound
Praises for the gift You are – You hold me close and dear.
Praises for the things you give like family, warmth and care.
I am really overwhelmed by Your goodness toward me.

There is no other Name above Your Name I know
And that is why there is, no other place to go.

***

Meltdown

ME: I may be very muddled, but one thing is quite clear. You are just the kind of person I hold very dear.

GOD: The rainbows are around you, even though you cannot see. My covenant surrounds you and I bid you, do not fear.

ME: My heart is breaking Lord. It is so very hurt. I wish that I could fix it, but I know that I cannot.

GOD: My daughter, I am with you. My loving arms surround. The angels sing their chorus, and you should see your crown.

ME: Does the crown now fix my heart and is my song so faint? Sometimes I do not hear the sounds, that the angels make.

GOD: My daughter, I am singing louder as My victory comes near. The giants in your life are coming down and down.

ME: Each time we fell a giant, there is another one, and I am weary Lord from all that we have done. How much longer Lord can I survive this test? It has been going on and on and I have given my best.

GOD: My daughter, I am good to you. You see Me all the time. How can you say 'I've nothing left' when all you have is Me? I am your all in all. I am your very breath. I am the One who heals you and gives you all My best. I see the darkness that you're in, but that's about to change. My Light is shining o'er the hill and one thing that I know, that Light will brighten up your path as soon as break of day. The morning bright and fair will fall upon you soon. The moon and stars will fade away at the dawning of the day.

ME: The night's been long – the warfare hard – but one thing I do know – My God is in control wherever I may go. Forgive me Lord for all my angst. I do not want to sin, but fire and ice have seared my soul and I feel emptiness within. There is not much reserve within my barren place. The only pleasure that I have is when I see Your face.

***

Surrender

Here in Your presence - Lord I will bring
All my concerns - You are my King
My sorrows and joy - the present and past,
My hopes and my fears - Lord I hold fast
To Your feet O my King.
My cares and my wares – to You they belong
Please don't give up – O Lord is my song
For richer, for poorer - in sickness and health
I pledge now my troth – to You I belong.

***

Grief

My grief it seems to have no bounds.
My grief it just goes round and around.
O Lord I wish to give it away, but I know,
You will make a way - A way of escape into new life.
Alone I feel – I give you my life.
I know You have a plan for me and it is one of liberty.
But through the pain – again I must go,
Weeping and wailing on this road below.
Lord I commit, my very being.
I'm shedding my tears and I feel like I'm bleeding.
My losses are great and my heart is on fire.
Lord help me, I plead, this very hour.

***

Dreams

Dreams are meant to be broken.
Dreams are meant to be lived.
Dreams are meant to inspire you.
But where do I fit in?
I am in a dilemma,
To know what my dream could be.
I've dreamt and dreamt and yet,
My dreams don't seem to be.

My dreams of life, so full and fair
With happy hours along life's way.
My dreams are shattered and yet,
Could there be another dream, waiting for me?
My dreams have come and gone.
Or so it would seem,
And yet, in God's great plan,
It seems my dreams do sleep.

Awake O sleeper and see the dawn.
Redeeming grace is here.
The love of God, so rich and rare,
Makes all my dreams so fair.
I dream of life so rich and new,
Of family near and far
How long O Lord before my dreams,
Come out into the air?

I know that you have promised
My dreams will be fulfilled,
But here I am O God,
At the crossroads once again.
My dreams they've been so many,
And my life has come and gone.
The endless years of trouble –
My dreams they seem long gone.

But You O Lord - You know my heart.
You know where I belong.
The dreams that have been shattered,
And new ones coming along.
O Lord My God, I stand in awe
And wonder, of how You work things out.

My life, my plans, my dreams, my all,
Are given at Your call,
To rest in peace, to lay me down,
At the mention of Your Name.

So, time has come and time has gone.
I am still upon the earth.
My life once over, has taken on rebirth.

***

Coming into Joy

You turn my mourning into dancing.
You turn my sorrow into joy.
But what does that mean O Lord
When I've known sorrow all my life?

What does joy look like? Where does the rainbow end?
Where does the sky begin? And how did I begin?
These questions are like the universe
That goes on and on and on
And yet, You have the answers.
They are founded in Your Word.

My life is like a vapour along with earth and sky and sea.
We all will pass away at the breaking of the new day.
Your new day O Lord is where everything is bright.
The roads are paved with gold and radiate Your Glorious Light.

I cannot wait to see me dancing boldly before Your Throne,
My heart so light and free of grief as You have promised me.
Joy unspeakable – full of Glory – is what Your Promise is,
And so, I wait on bended knee, and expect to see,
That Promise, to be fulfilled in me.

***

Midnight Alert

I am alert in the Spirit – Hallowed be Thy Name
I am alert in the Spirit – He calls me by my name
I am alert in the Spirit – It is the midnight hour
I am alert in the Spirit – And I know it is His power.

My sleep is taken from me – His voice I long to hear
My spirit is awake and I am seeking Him this hour.
What do You say O Lord My God, as I give to You My all.
How can I best serve You at what some would say,
Is such an ungodly hour.

But You O Lord are not bound by time,
My spirit knows full well.
The writing's on the wall and it says that all is well.
For You are in control of things, both day and night,
And my heart, it listens for You, in the middle of the night.

You walk about so softly and yet You sometimes roar,
But in the middle of the night, Your whisper is so small.
I long to hear You call my name no matter night or day
I answer YES to You what e'er the time may be
For You O Lord are my companion and only a breath away.

I love to sing to You, and I love to hear Your song
It is just as if two love birds are singing all day long.
The kindness of Your heart – the love You have for me
Is all I want to know e'en though You show Your power.

I know I'm not forsaken. I sense Your Presence near.
My spirit is alert at this midnight hour.
I thank You for the day. I thank You for the night.
It makes no difference to You, for You are always Light.
So I humbly bow before You and I worship You alone
As I lay me down to sleep – I know I'm not alone.

***

Hope Realized

My hope stands in Jesus Blood and His righteousness.
The sky has parted – the Red Sea closed
I stand on Holy Ground in a brand new place.
The enemies that once stood near
Are buried beneath the miry clay.

My hope, it is in Christ alone
There can be no one else.
The future is in His strong hands
Along with me, His child of grace.

My hope is built on nothing less
Than the promises of God – which are blessed.
His truth prevails – His promise sure
This much we know – It will endure.

Thru endless days and endless nights
Our God – He always wins the fight.
He blesses prayer and our surrender.
He manifests Himself in splendour.

There is no other God – He is the God of generations.
Abraham, Isaac, Jacob – Parent, children, grandchildren.
His works revealed – His Name adored.
There is no one else Who Keeps His Word.

***

Healing Grief

When the grief, it is so deep, and there is sadness all around
It's going to take a miracle, to get me off the ground.
It really is surprising what a year or two can do
When the love for one another – is taken away from you.
This love still lingers – the pain's still there -
How does one resolve it – when there's laughter in the air.

The tension is so great. Yet, the tension, is also fine.
It's like a spider's web of silk – that makes it so divine.

But My Lord – He likes to whisper. His words so soft and fair,
My daughter – he is with Me,
Even though he's not down there.
I know he's better off in Heaven – His sickness now no more
But that doesn't stop me missing him
And his eyes with love to share.

Sometimes the pain is great. Sometimes it isn't there
Or maybe it's just hiding, when I'm busy with my cares.

O Lord, I need Your healing touch
For which I thank You very much.
You are my healing grace
And so I rest in You right now
As I receive Your healing touch.
My life transformed - my vision clear
It changes all the atmosphere.

***

The Other Side

Over on the other side, the other side,
On the other side, over on the other side,
That's where the beauty of the Lord is.
The beauty of the Lord - The beauty of the Lord.
The beauty of the Lord is on the other side.

On the sides of the North
That's where the beauty of the Lord is.
The beauty of the Lord – It's on the other side.
The Glory of the Great King is on the other side.

We see the beauty of the Great King.
We see the Glory of the Great King on the other side.
None can compare to the beauty
And the Glory of the Great King on the other side.
None can compare to the Power of the Great King
On the other side.
None can compare to the Name of the King
As we pass to the other side.

The Name above all Names – The King above all Kings
The Glory of His Name – The Power of His Name
None can compare and none can compete
As we cross to the other side.

We bow this side and on the other side
At the Name of our King.
We give our lives on this side and the other side.
To Him we give Glory – To Him we give Praise
As we proclaim His Name – As we proclaim His Name.

***

Starting Anew

Here we go again
Starting with a brand new grin.
My grin, it is from ear to ear.
My face, it does not have a tear.
My face is washed. My hair is clean.
My Lord – it is on Him I lean.

He does not do things by halves.
He completes the picture He desires.
My Lord – His cross to bear.
It is at this cross where I lay my tears.

I rise again. New hope is here.
I wonder if I should shed a tear.
The new has come. The old is gone
And the joy has only just begun.

My Saviour's face I do behold.
My Saviour's hand I love to hold.
My Saviour's love I do receive.
My Saviour has His hand on me.

***

Tearful Memories

Painful memories one by one
Come to the surface when day is done.
Upon my soul they do alight
When all I want, is to sleep at night.

I wish these memories would fade away.
They're always there even through the day.
They are suppressed as I do my work
But at night they come when I would rest.

My tears, they are not gone,
Even though life moves along.
I do my best to brush them aside,
But sometimes, they are more than I can abide.
I long for the Lord to come to my aid,
He said He would wipe all tears away.
The past, it holds, just so much pain,
And I know that in Heaven there is no pain.
I feel betwixt and between,
The past and future gain.

I long for release and yet
I must hang on for my life has purpose.
It is not time for me to die yet.

I have work to do in my Master's Name.
It is my job to bring Him fame.
To tell out my story and His grace toward me,
As I journey through life – His Presence so dear.

I will tell of His love.
I will tell of His joy.
I will tell of His greatness
And His deliverance so free.

***

Dad

My dad has gone – The Lord has come
And taken him to his new home
No longer on earth but in Heaven above
A new life begins.

We below are left to mourn
But not as the heathen do
For once again will we unite
At the coming of the dawn.

Farewell, Au revoir, Goodbye
Until we meet again
In God's good time – by God's great grace
We will see each other again.

***

Musing

Here and now I'm in great pain,
What will it be like when I'm 99?
Will I be in Heaven with my Saviour so dear
Or still on the earth battling fear?

My life like a vapour is floating away
But 70 odd years does not seem old
In comparison to the eternity roll
As the ages come and go.

***

Consecration

All my days and all my hours, I surrender to You Lord.
All my days and all my hours, I choose to love You Lord.
All my days and all my hours, I choose to serve You Lord.

All my life is Yours O Lord
Whatever the cost may be.
I choose to have You in my life
Even though it could cause strife.
My neighbours and my friends may not concur with me,
But You O Lord are, a good friend to me.

The rest is up to you O Lord
To show yourself to me,
To set me on a path which leads
Directly up to You.

Take my life. I consecrate it Lord to You.
Fill my days with praise and honour to Your Name.
Cause me always to bring Your Name to fame.
It's not by might, nor by my own power.
It can only be achieved by Your Spirit's Power.
Your Life in mine and my life in You
It is the only way to go.

***

Looking for Love

Here I am again Lord, looking for Your face.
I believe You brought me here
To heal me in this place.
I am looking for Your love – the fiery, blazing love
That flows out from – Your awesome throne above.
I am looking for Your passion Lord to fill my heart anew,
So I can be Your hands and feet while I am on the earth.
I am looking for Your heart – to join with my own heart
So that all that is of You will become
All I want of You.
I am looking for Your power to adorn my life afresh
For with Your love and power
I can do all that You would wish.
My heart is Yours O Lord to fill and fill again
To overflow my life with Your compassion,
For the sons of men.

***

The Majesty of Love

We give praise to You only, as we walk along each day.
We see the majesty of the sky and the waters break.
The waves they come and the waves they go.
They crash upon the shore and then they are no more.
Your Majesty O Lord – my soul, it will be filled.

I see Your Majesty, O Lord, in all that You have made,
The sky, the sea – the rocks upon the shore.
Your breakers O Lord, as they crash into my life
Leave me breathless and wanting more.
Overflow me with Your Love. Fill me to my core.

Your Love O Lord is like a diamond. It sparkles in the Light.
I need Your Love O Lord, to fill my darkest night.
My need of You is great and You are greatly to be praised.
How can my need be filled unless I'm filled by You?

Only by Your Spirit Lord will I be filled again.
The loneliness – the emptiness – Come Lord. Come again.
Fill me with Your Love – the essence of Your Being.
Empower me with Your Love so I can live for You,
Knowing Who You are to me, in this very hour.

I will give praise to You O Lord My God,
My Prophet, Priest and King.
To live for You, empowered by Love, to rise and live again.
Your resurrection power O Lord, it is within my reach
But I must wait for You My Lord,
As You, my heart would teach.

I sit here at Your feet O Lord, to see Your hand reach out
To touch my life – to stir my heart and lift me to new heights.
I am Your daughter Lord – a maid servant I would be,
To serve You all my days and through Eternity.

***

Come Lord

You are my Rock, my Fortress, my Life.
You are the One I seek.
I lay down my life before You Lord.
Come be my Help I pray.

Come be the Life I so long for.
Come be my Everything.
Come be my Light, my Jesus.
As all on the altar I lay.

Come be my Lord, my Song,
As into the darkness I sing.
Come be the One Who enriches me,
As all on the altar I lay.

Come be my Life, my Joy, my Song,
As here in this place I wait.
Come to me Lord in a fresh new way.
Come be my All in All this day.

Come be my Light, my Life, my All.
Come to this place I pray.
Come knocking O Lord and I will answer,
In this place today.

Come where I'm at – away from home.
Come and refresh me I pray.
Come and anoint me with oil again,
So I can function each day.

COME LORD COME. I'm desperate for You.
I want You to come today.
I'm waiting for You, My Lord, my God,
To fill my life afresh this day.

***

My Turn

When is it my turn O Lord? When is it my turn
To know the love and peace that passes all understanding?
When is it my turn O Lord, for the ocean of Your love
To consume me, overtake me and flow over me?
When is it my turn?

When is it my turn for Your healing power to overcome me?
When is it my turn for Your healing power
To flow through me?
I see others moving forward, flowing in their destiny.
When is it my turn?

It is my time. I know it is. But You O Lord withhold.
Am I not there? Have I got it wrong? Where is MY song?
I know that You exist. I know that You are here.
When is it my turn O Lord? I ask. Where do I fit in?
When is it my turn?

***

Reality Check

The holiday is over. To home I must return.
Home seems so far away and yet it is so dear.
My days here are fulfilled. The Lord, He is so near
As I wait to travel home with friends who care.

The Lord, He is so real. He never leaves my side.
I follow after Him – with Him I will abide.
My hopes and dreams are not shattered.
My faith, it rises still. I see the coming of the Lord
And I run to meet Him, on His Holy hill.

The Lord, He is my all. He is my dearest friend.
I know He will be with me to the very end.
I shall not fear the way. His Light, it leads me on.
My journey I will take – with Him my closest friend.

I shall not fear the battle, for He is by my side.
He shall come for me – if I in Him abide.
His promises are sure – He is Yes and Amen.
It is surely time, to meet with Him again.

He shows His lovely face and His glory does abound.
I will trust in Him, and then in Him, I'm found.

***

This New Day

The new day is here. It has finally dawned.
It did not come with fanfare or push through in a storm.
It came so quietly in the natural and My God has great plans.
He has given us another day – a day unlike any other.
A day to give Him thanks and praise His Holy Name.
A day to witness His great love and to love Him in return.

A new day – O what bliss
A new day – one that we will kiss.
His blessing is upon us – His joy, it fills our hearts.
This new day – what a day
Heaven is rejoicing
The new is here – the old is gone.
Hallelujah!

***

Come and Sing

This is the new day – COME – let us sing to the Lord
This is the new day – COME – let us praise His Name
This is the new day – COME – let us join ourselves to Him.

This is the new day – COME!

This is the new day and I will sing to the Lord
This is the new day and I will sing to the One I adore

This is the new day – SING a new song to praise His Name

SING - a new song.

SING – of His greatness and sing of His love
SING – of the joy in Heaven above
SING – of His ways so righteous and pure
SING – of His peace He bestows upon us

SING!

SING – songs of deliverance so great
SING – of His freedom in this very hour
SING – of His love and sing of His power
SING – of His Presence in this day and hour.

SING! COME AND SING!

***

Now He who searches the hearts knows what the mind of the Spirit is, because He makes intercession for the saints according to the will of God. And we know that all things work together for good to those who love God, to those who are called according to His purpose.

Romans 8:27-28 NKJV